picture This!

Mick Gowar

OXFORD
UNIVERSITY PRESS

OXFORD
UNIVERSITY PRESS

is a department of the University of Oxford.
It furthers the University's objective of excellence in research, scholarship,
and education by publishing worldwide in

Oxford   New York

Auckland   Cape Town   Dar es Salaam   Hong Kong   Karachi
Kuala Lumpur   Madrid   Melbourne   Mexico City   Nairobi
New Delhi   Shanghai   Taipei   Toronto

With offices in

Argentina   Austria   Brazil   Chile   Czech Republic   France   Greece
Guatemala   Hungary   Italy   Japan   Poland   Portugal   Singapore
South Korea   Switzerland   Thailand   Turkey   Ukraine   Vietnam

Oxford is a registered trade mark of Oxford University Press
in the UK and in certain other countries

British Library Cataloguing in Publication Data

Data available

ISBN: 978-0-19-846133-3

5 7 9 10 8 6 4

Printed in China by Imago

Paper used in the production of this book is a natural,
recyclable product made from wood grown in sustainable forests.
The manufacturing process conforms to the environmental
regulations of the country of origin.

Acknowledgements

The publisher would like to thank the following for permission to reproduce photographs: **p5**b OUP/Chris
Honeywell, **p6** Ghost Stories cover – Reproduced from Stories of Ghosts by permission of Usborne Publishing,
83–85 Saffron Hill, London ECIN 8RT, UK Copyright © 2004 Usborne Publishing Ltd, **p7**t Rex Features/Kenny Elrick,
p8 OUP/Chris Honeywell, **p9** OUP/Chris Honeywell, **p11**t Squeezes from Gargling with Jelly by Brian Patten/Puffin
Books/Rogers Coleridge & White, b Art Archive Library/Kandinsky Vasily, composition VIII ADAGP, Paris, and DACS,
London, 2006, **p13** OUP/Chris Honeywell, **p14** One Ballerina Two cover illustration © 1991 Jan Ormerod From ONE
BALLERINA TWO by Vivian French & illustrated by Jan Ormerod. Reproduced by permission of Walker Books Ltd,
London SE11 5HJ, **p15**t Sunshine cover – Sunshine by Jan Ormerod published by Frances Lincoln limited copyright
© Jan Ormerod 1981. Reproduced by permission of Frances Lincoln b the Dancing Class c1873–76 (oil on canvas) by
Degas, Edgar (1834–1917) © Musee d'Orsay, Paris/the Bridgeman Art Library, **p17** OUP/Chris Honeywell, **p18** main
photo: Kettles Yard, University of Cambridge, **p21**t Saltash (oil and w/c on board) by Wallis, Alfred (1855–1942) ©
Kettles Yard, University of Cambridge, UK/The Bridgeman Art Library b 'This is Sain Fishery That Used To Be', St Ives
Harbour and Godrevy Lighthouse (oil on board) by Wallis, Alfred (1855–1942) © Barbara Hepworth Museum and
Sculpture Garden, St Ives, UK/The Bridgeman Art Library

Thanks to Mick Gowar, Mike Phillips, David Mostyn and Jan Ormerod for supplying all other photographs

Cover: Chris Honeywell

Illustrations by David Mostyn: **p22**, **p23**

Designed by Bigtop

Contents

Introduction

This is a book about people who make pictures.

"My name's Mike and I draw cartoons. I also draw pictures for the *Horrible History* and *Geography* books."

"Hi! I'm David and I've always loved drawing comics."

"I'm Jan. I draw and paint pictures for books, and I also write the stories."

"My name's Julia. I work in an art gallery, helping children to learn more about making pictures."

This is also a book about *you* and the pictures you make. In this book you'll find some great tips from these artists on how you can make your pictures more interesting.

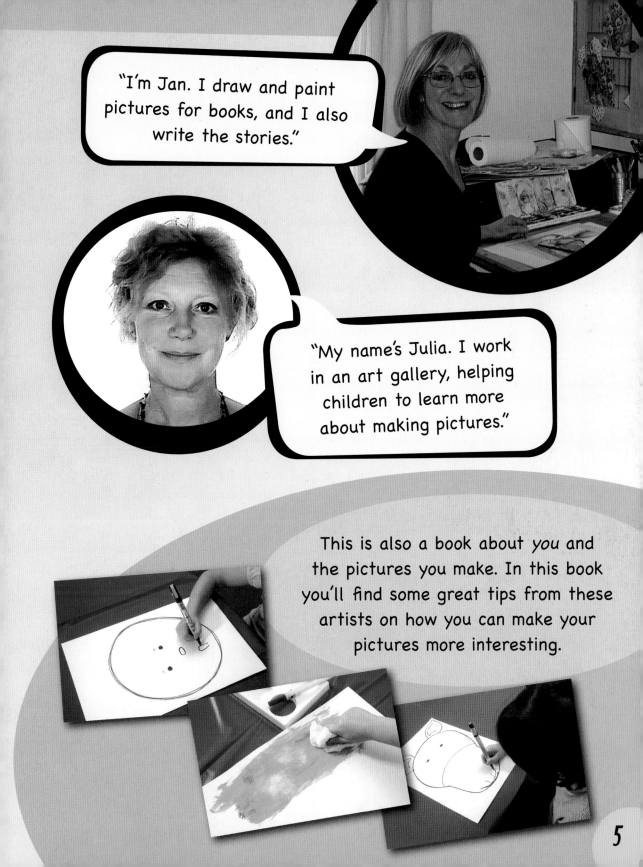

Mike Phillips

"I started drawing when I was very young – before I went to school. The first picture I remember drawing was of a parrot. My aunt thought it was so good she kept it on her wall for 30 years!

After I left school I worked in a small printing firm before becoming a cartoonist. I sent cartoons to newspapers and magazines and drew pictures for birthday cards."

USBORNE YOUNG READING
Stories of
GHOSTS

TreeTops All Stars
BEASTLY
Basil
Tessa Krailing

Horrible Geography
DESPERATE DESERTS
ANITA GANERI
HE REALLY GIVES ME THE HUMP!

Star Artist

"My star artist is Quentin Blake. I like the sketchy way he draws, and the colours he uses. All his books look really lively and exciting."

Pick of my books

"I love illustrating history books. I do a lot of research to make sure the clothes are right."

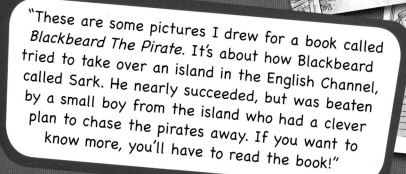

"These are some pictures I drew for a book called *Blackbeard The Pirate*. It's about how Blackbeard tried to take over an island in the English Channel, called Sark. He nearly succeeded, but was beaten by a small boy from the island who had a clever plan to chase the pirates away. If you want to know more, you'll have to read the book!"

Hot tips!

"Practise drawing as much as you can. Start with yourself. Draw yourself in a mirror. Pull faces."

"Draw yourself looking:

- happy
- sad
- angry."

"In cartoons you often have to give animals human expressions and feelings. It's not easy, because most animal faces have one thing humans don't: a snout. But practise and you'll get the hang of it."

"Follow these stages:

1. Draw a circle for the face, as you would for a cartoon of a human.
2. Next add the snout – long for a horse, round for a cat, more pointed for a dog.
3. Now add the eyes, eyebrows and mouth to show the expression:
   - big eyes, raised eyebrows and a small mouth to show surprise
   - raised eyebrows, small eyes and a wide mouth for happiness
   - heavy, frowning eyebrows, big eyes and teeth to show anger."

Jan Ormerod

"I grew up in Western Australia. My father worked for an oil company. We moved from town to town, living in one place for about four years and then moving on again."

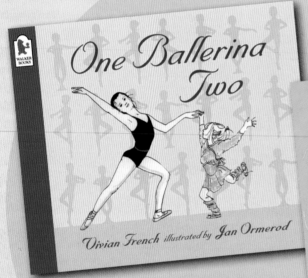

"I drew all the time when I was a child. I drew everything. I practised drawing all the time. My favourite things to draw were ballerinas and skaters (that looked like Barbie dolls) and horses. I started writing and illustrating books when I came to live in England."

Pick of my books

Sunshine — Jan Ormerod

"My first two books, *Sunshine* and *Moonlight*, had stories but no words. I used my husband and my daughter, Sophie, as models. I posed them, took photographs and then drew from the photographs."

"I sometimes use friends as models, too."

Star Artist

"My star artist is Edgar Degas. He painted the ordinary movements of dancers and horses so well that you almost believe they are alive in the picture."

Hot tips!

"There are no rules that say you can only use a brush or a pencil or a pen to make a picture. I use whatever I think will make the marks I want. I've used sticks, bits of cotton wool, old toothbrushes and sponges.

For my book, *Lizzie Nonsense*, I used sponges a lot. In this picture, Lizzie's Dad is driving a wagon and horses along a dusty road."

"There are tall trees and bushes beside the road. I used sponges to paint the leaves and trees and to make the dust cloud the horses are kicking up."

"There are two quite different ways to get this effect. You can:

1. Dip a sponge into thick paint.

2. Remove most of the paint by pressing the sponge onto a piece of paper or tissue.

3. Press the sponge onto your paper.

or
1. Put thin watercolour paint onto your picture in the usual way with a brush.

2. Press a dry sponge or piece of tissue onto the wet paint.

3. Lift the sponge or tissue off."

Julia Tozer

"I work at Kettle's Yard in Cambridge. It was once the home of a man named Jim Ede. Jim collected paintings and sculptures. He wanted to share his art collection with lots of people. So, when he was old, he moved out so that other people could enjoy his home and art."

"This is the special room in Kettle's Yard where children can make pictures and sculptures. Sometimes artists come to help the children."

> "We have lots of events for children."

'Glitter and Glue' drop-in sessions

10 AUGUST, 14 SEPTEMBER 10.00–11.30

Monthly drop-in art sessions for pre-school children and their carers. Just come and have fun making whatever you want.

'Junk Sculpture' with Tom Karen

2 AUGUST 10.30–13.00

For 5–8 year olds

Tom will help you make a 3D work out of scrap materials and there will be a chance to decorate it, too.

Helen Kenny's Plaster Workshop

15 AUGUST 11.45–13.45

For 8–12 year olds

Look at different ways of making sculptures in the house at Kettle's Yard. Design a mould using Plasticine and take a cast from it.

"This is our Wednesday Club for children aged 8–11."

Star Artist

"My star artist is Alfred Wallis. He lived by the sea. He left school when he was only 9 years old to work as a fisherman. He didn't start painting until he was over 70. He painted things he could remember from when he was a boy.

He didn't have much money, so he painted on old pieces of wood he found on the beach, or old bits of cardboard and empty porridge boxes. Alfred didn't use the sort of paints artists normally use. He used paint boat-builders use to paint ships, or the sort of paint people use to paint walls and woodwork in their houses."

How *this* book was made

A book about art and illustration would be great.

Mick teaches in an art school and writes books for children. He would be a good author to write the book.

This book would be more interesting if real artists talk about their work – and gave tips to the readers on making pictures.

Mick makes a plan.

SOB! HE MAY NEVER RETURN!

ARTISTS

Annemarie is the editor of TreeTops non-fiction. She needs new ideas.

Mick goes off to interview the illustrators, Jan, David and Mike.

"Not too many words. Lots of room on the page for pictures – it is a book about pictures!"

Mick starts writing.

The editor checks Mick's draft.

It's the job of the art editor and picture researcher to find the pictures.

The designer puts together the words and pictures so every page looks exciting to read.

Now the book can be printed.

The sales rep calls into a primary school with the new Tree Tops book.

Mrs Nyman shows her class their new books.

Index